TO

_____

ON

_____

FROM

_____

Kregel's
CHRISTMAS
TREASURY
OF
ILLUSTRATED
BIBLE
STORIES

MATT LOCKHART

General Editor

KREGEL
CHILDREN'S

Kregel's Christmas Treasury of Illustrated Bible Stories
© 2023 by Classic Bible Art, LLC

Published by Kregel Publications, a division of Kregel Inc., 2450 Oak Industrial Dr. NE, Grand Rapids, MI 49505. www.kregel.com.

Cataloging-in-Publication Data is available from the Library of Congress.

ISBN 978-0-8254-4832-4

Printed in China
23 24 25 26 27 28 29 30 31 32 / 5 4 3 2 1

Contents

A Note to Parents

Welcome to *Kregel's Christmas Treasury of Illustrated Bible Stories*! I'm excited to share these wonderful stories and illustrations with you.

Inside these pages you will find eighteen episodes that portray the key events surrounding the advent of Christ's birth. Each story in this family keepsake is attractively laid out and beautifully adorned with classic fine art. Additionally, there are a dozen ideas sprinkled throughout to help your family enjoy the season and experience the true meaning of Christmas. As a bonus, there's also an Advent Bible reading plan in the back of this book you can follow as you count down the days leading up to Christmas.

While many Bible storybooks retell stories, I have compiled text from actual Scripture! I have used a variety of respected modern translations to render each episode in a way that is easy to read and understand. The verses printed in this book are referenced at the end of each Scripture passage, along with the designated translation abbreviation as noted on the copyright page.

Since nothing can replace the value of reading from your own Bible, I encourage you to explore these stories further in the Word and in full context by reading for yourself the chapters from which the episodes are taken. Encourage your children or grandchildren to read the Bible independently as well. Starting this practice at a young age helps kids know God and establish the important habit of regular Bible reading.

Matt

About the Artwork

The wonderful illustrations featured throughout this volume come from one of the largest privately held collections of vintage Bible art. The art was originally commissioned by Standard Publishing, in pursuit of providing high quality illustrations to complement their Sunday school materials. Some of the works featured in this book date back to more than one hundred years ago, as the collection came together over a period of about fifty years, with the latest pieces dating to the late 1950s.

Within the overall collection, there is artwork attributed to more than fifty different artists. Of the illustrations featured in this book, several are credited to two American artists, Cleveland Woodward and Otto Stemler.

Cleveland Woodward (1900–1985): Born in Glendale, Ohio, and a graduate of the Cincinnati Art Academy, Cleveland continued his training in Europe, studying at the British Academy of Art in Rome. He also spent time in the Holy Land and was known for his Bible illustrations.

Otto Stemler (1872–1953): Born in Cincinnati, Ohio, Otto studied at the Cincinnati Art Academy and was Standard's primary in-house artist. He made artistic contributions to the collection over the span of a forty-year career. His works often feature bold colors.

❧ ❧

Matt Lockhart has spent nearly three decades in ministry and Christian publishing and enjoys creating books that help children and adults get into the Bible.

The Promise of a Savior

"The days are coming," declares the LORD,
   "when I will raise up for David a righteous Branch,
a King who will reign wisely
   and do what is just and right in the land.
In his days Judah will be saved
   and Israel will live in safety.
This is the name by which he will be called:
   The LORD Our Righteous Savior."

Jeremiah 23:5–6 (NIV)

As you count down the days until Christmas, consider incorporating the Advent Bible reading plan on page 45 into your daily routine. There is a short reading for each day from December 1 to Christmas Day.

An Angel Appears to Zechariah

When Herod was king of Judea, there was a Jewish priest named Zechariah. He was a member of the priestly order of Abijah, and his wife, Elizabeth, was also from the priestly line of Aaron.

They had no children because Elizabeth was unable to conceive, and they were both very old.

One day Zechariah was serving God in the Temple, for his order was on duty that week.

While Zechariah was in the sanctuary, an angel of the Lord appeared to him, standing to the right of the incense altar. Zechariah was shaken and overwhelmed with fear when he saw him. But the angel said, "Don't be afraid, Zechariah! God has heard your prayer. Your wife, Elizabeth, will give you a son, and you are to name him John.

"He will be a man with the spirit and power of Elijah. He will prepare the people for the coming of the Lord."

Luke 1:5, 7–8, 11–13, 17 (NLT)

An Angel Appears to Mary

During Elizabeth's sixth month of pregnancy, God sent the angel Gabriel to a virgin who lived in Nazareth, a town in Galilee. She was engaged to marry a man named Joseph from the family of David. Her name was Mary. The angel came to her and said, "Greetings! The Lord has blessed you and is with you."

But Mary was very confused by what the angel said. Mary wondered, "What does this mean?"

The angel said to her, "Don't be afraid, Mary, because God is pleased with you. Listen! You will become pregnant. You will give birth to a son, and you will name him Jesus."

Mary said to the angel, "How will this happen? I am a virgin!"

The angel said to Mary, "The Holy Spirit will come upon you, and the power of the Most High will cover you. The baby will be holy. He will be called the Son of God. Now listen! Elizabeth, your relative, is very old. But she is also pregnant with a son. Everyone thought she could not have a baby, but she has been pregnant for six months. God can do everything!"

Luke 1:26–31, 34–37 (ICB)

Making homemade decorations is a fun way to get into the Christmas spirit. Colorful paper chains and snowflakes are easy to make. Gather scissors, paper, and glue, and turn on some Christmas music. Tape snowflakes in a window or string the paper chain around the tree.

Mary Visits Elizabeth

Mary got up and went quickly to a town in the hills of Judea. She came to Zechariah's house and greeted Elizabeth. When Elizabeth heard Mary's greeting, the unborn baby inside her jumped, and Elizabeth was filled with the Holy Spirit. She cried out in a loud voice, "God has blessed you more than any other woman, and he has blessed the baby to which you will give birth. Why has this good thing happened to me, that the mother of my Lord comes to me? When I heard your voice, the baby inside me jumped with joy. You are blessed because you believed that what the Lord said to you would really happen."

Mary stayed with Elizabeth for about three months and then returned home.

Luke 1:39–45, 56 (NCV)

In addition to or in place of creating a Christmas list, consider a new tradition: writing short thank-you notes to Jesus. After sharing your notes together as a family, tuck them in the Christmas tree or display them next to the nativity or somewhere in your home.

The Birth of John the Baptist

When the time came for Elizabeth to have her child, she gave birth to a son. Her neighbors and relatives heard that the Lord had been very kind to her, and they shared her joy.

When the child was eight days old, they went to the temple to circumcise him. They were going to name him Zechariah after his father. But his mother spoke up, "Absolutely not! His name will be John."

Their friends said to her, "But you don't have any relatives with that name."

So they motioned to the baby's father to see what he wanted to name the child. Zechariah asked for a writing tablet and wrote, "His name is John." Everyone was amazed.

Suddenly, Zechariah was able to speak, and he began to praise God.

Luke 1:57–64 (GW)

Enjoy an evening walk or drive, taking in the Christmas lights and decorations in your neighborhood. Some towns also host a parade of lights, which can be fun for all ages.

An Angel Appears to Joseph

This is how Jesus Christ was born. A young woman named Mary was engaged to Joseph from King David's family. But before they were married, she learned that she was going to have a baby by God's Holy Spirit. Joseph was a good man and did not want to embarrass Mary in front of everyone. So he decided to quietly call off the wedding.

While Joseph was thinking about this, an angel from the Lord appeared to him in a dream. The angel said, "Joseph, the baby that Mary will have is from the Holy Spirit. Go ahead and marry her. Then after her baby is born, name him Jesus, because he will save his people from their sins."

Matthew 1:18–21 (CEV)

Mary and Joseph Go to Bethlehem

At that time the Roman emperor, Augustus, decreed that a census should be taken throughout the Roman Empire. (This was the first census taken when Quirinius was governor of Syria.) All returned to their own ancestral towns to register for this census. And because Joseph was a descendant of King David, he had to go to Bethlehem in Judea, David's ancient home. He traveled there from the village of Nazareth in Galilee. He took with him Mary, to whom he was engaged, who was now expecting a child.

Luke 2:1–5 (NLT)

The Birth of Jesus

While they were in Bethlehem, the time came for Mary to have her child. She gave birth to her firstborn son. She wrapped him in strips of cloth and laid him in a manger because there wasn't any room for them in the inn.

Luke 2:6–7 (GW)

Have a family sleepover near the Christmas tree. As part of the evening, turn off phones and electronic devices and instead read Christmas books together or play board games. When it's time to turn in, share with each other one thing you're thankful for. Perhaps cozy beds might top your list.

The Shepherds Receive Good News

There were shepherds living out in the fields nearby. It was night, and they were taking care of their sheep. An angel of the Lord appeared to them. And the glory of the Lord shone around them. They were terrified. But the angel said to them, "Do not be afraid. I bring you good news. It will bring great joy for all the people. Today in the town of David a Savior has been born to you. He is the Messiah, the Lord. Here is how you will know I am telling you the truth. You will find a baby wrapped in strips of cloth and lying in a manger."

Luke 2:8–12 (NIrV)

Pop some corn, mix up some hot cocoa, and select a favorite Christmas movie to enjoy together as a family. *A Charlie Brown Christmas* is a classic and even features Linus quoting Luke 2:8–14. What a great way to relay the true meaning of Christmas!

An Angel Choir

Suddenly a great army of heaven's angels appeared with the angel, singing praises to God:

"Glory to God in the highest heaven,
and peace on earth to those with whom he is pleased!"

Luke 2:13–14 (GNT)

Think of a special friend or family member who lives far away. As a family, preselect two or three favorite Christmas songs to practice together before scheduling a video call with this person. Then surprise them with long-distance virtual caroling.

The Shepherds Visit Jesus

When the angels left them and went back to heaven, the shepherds said to each other, "Let's go to Bethlehem. Let's see this thing that has happened which the Lord has told us about."

So the shepherds went quickly and found Mary and Joseph and the baby, who was lying in a feeding trough. When they had seen him, they told what the angels had said about this child.

Then the shepherds went back to their sheep, praising God and thanking him for everything they had seen and heard. It had been just as the angel had told them.

Luke 2:15–17, 20 (NCV)

Mary and Baby Jesus

All who heard the shepherds' story were astonished, but Mary kept all these things in her heart and thought about them often.

Luke 2:18–19 (NLT)

Make plans to attend a Christmas pageant or Christmas Eve service as a family. Together choose at least one person to invite to join you. Think about someone you know who might not be able to go on their own, or perhaps someone new to the area who doesn't have anyone to go with.

Jesus Presented in the Temple

The time came for Joseph and Mary to perform the ceremony of purification, as the Law of Moses commanded. So they took the child to Jerusalem to present him to the Lord, as it is written in the law of the Lord: "Every first-born male is to be dedicated to the Lord." They also went to offer a sacrifice of a pair of doves or two young pigeons, as required by the law of the Lord.

Luke 2:22–24 (GNT)

Did someone say Christmas cookies? Involve the family in age- and skill-appropriate ways, from mixing the ingredients to decorating, to taste testing, to delivering a batch to a friend or neighbor. If a grandparent lives nearby, involve them in the fun as well.

The Child of Promise Proclaimed

In Jerusalem there was a man named Simeon. He was a good and godly man. He was waiting for God's promise to Israel to come true. The Holy Spirit was with him. The Spirit had told Simeon that he would not die before he had seen the Lord's Messiah. The Spirit led him into the temple courtyard. Then Jesus' parents brought the child in. They came to do for him what the Law required. Simeon took Jesus in his arms and praised God. He said,

> "Lord, you are the King over all.
>> Now let me, your servant, go in peace.
>> That is what you promised.
> My eyes have seen your salvation."

There was also a prophet named Anna. She was the daughter of Penuel from the tribe of Asher. Anna was very old. After getting married, she lived with her husband seven years. Then she was a widow until she was 84. She never left the temple. She worshiped night and day, praying and going without food. Anna came up to Jesus' family at that moment. She gave thanks to God. And she spoke about the child to all who were looking forward to the time when Jerusalem would be set free.

Luke 2:25–30, 36–38 (NIrv)

Journey of the Wise Men

Jesus was born in the town of Bethlehem in Judea during the time when Herod was king. After Jesus was born, some wise men from the east came to Jerusalem. They asked, "Where is the baby who was born to be the king of the Jews? We saw his star in the east. We came to worship him."

Matthew 2:1–2 (ICB)

Plan ahead and deliver a special treat to someone who has to work on Christmas Eve. It can be as simple as dropping off a box of donuts or a batch of homemade goodies to a fire station or giving a gift card or handcrafted ornament to a driver making deliveries on your street.

The Wise Men Before Herod

Then Herod had a secret meeting with the wise men and learned from them the exact time they first saw the star. He sent the wise men to Bethlehem, saying, "Look carefully for the child. When you find him, come tell me so I can worship him too."

Matthew 2:7–8 (NCV)

The Wise Men Visit Jesus

After the Wise Men had listened to the king, they went on their way. The star they had seen when it rose went ahead of them. It finally stopped over the place where the child was. When they saw the star, they were filled with joy. The Wise Men went to the house. There they saw the child with his mother Mary. They bowed down and worshiped him. Then they opened their treasures. They gave him gold, frankincense and myrrh. But God warned them in a dream not to go back to Herod. So they returned to their country on a different road.

Matthew 2:9–12 (NIrv)

You may not have any spare gold, frankincense, or myrrh, but consider giving what you can to those in need. Involve the whole family in purchasing food, winter clothing, toys, or books to donate to a local ministry or organization. Pray a blessing over the gifts, and deliver them together.

God's Christmas Gift for You!

For God so loved the world, that he gave his only begotten Son, that whosoever believeth in him should not perish, but have everlasting life.

John 3:16 (AKJV)

Jesus entered the world as a baby on that first Christmas because God loves you and gave you the gift of a Savior. What a wonderful Christmas gift! And what do you do with a gift? You receive it and it becomes yours. When you accept the gift of Jesus by believing in him, salvation, forgiveness, everlasting life, and a relationship with God all become yours. If you're not sure what this means, talk about it with your mom or dad or someone you know who loves Jesus. Together you can pray: *Dear God, thank you for sending Jesus to earth to die for my sins and to be my Savior. I believe in Jesus and want to have a relationship with you. Thank you for the best gift ever. Amen.*

Advent Bible Reading Plan

As you count down the days from December 1 to Christmas Day, here's a Bible reading plan you can use. Reading these passages can help you and your family prepare for Christmas by further reflecting on the true meaning of Christ's birth.

The Prophets Tell of the Messiah

December 1: Isaiah 9:1–6
December 2: Isaiah 11:1–10
December 3: Isaiah 35:1–10
December 4: Isaiah 40:1–11
December 5: Isaiah 61:1–4, 8–11
December 6: Isaiah 64:1–9
December 7: Jeremiah 23:1–6
December 8: Micah 5:1–4

The Angel Gabriel Appears

December 9: Luke 1:5–25
December 10: Luke 1:26–38
December 11: Luke 1:39–56

John the Baptist, Forerunner of Christ

December 12: Luke 1:57–66
December 13: Luke 1:67–80
December 14: Mark 1:2–8
December 15: Luke 3:7–18
December 16: John 1:19–27
December 17: Matthew 11:2–15

Jesus, the Promised Messiah

December 18: John 1:1–5, 10–18
December 19: Matthew 1:18–25
December 20: Luke 2:1–8
December 21: Luke 2:9–20
December 22: Luke 2:21–40
December 23: Matthew 2:1–12
December 24: Matthew 2:13, 19–23

God's Gift to You

December 25: John 3:16–21

Continue the Tradition

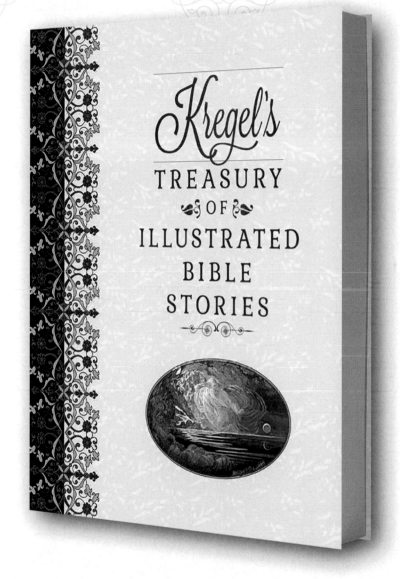

This richly designed, high-quality hardcover is ideal for Easter, kindergarten graduations, baptisms, and other gift-giving occasions. With 250 stories pulled straight from the text of Scripture, *Kregel's Illustrated Treasury of Bible Stories* is destined to become a cherished family classic.